The Lucy Maxym Collection
of Russian Lacquer

1. SHOWN ON COVER. RUSLAN AND LUDMILLA PALEKH

Three artists collaborated on this magnificent work, which was commissioned in 1985 and completed in 1987. The left panel painted by Y. Shanitsin, shows Ludmilla being abducted from her father's house by the sorcerer, Chernomor. As she is being borne away in the sky, we see her three suitors galloping off to her rescue. The middle panel, painted by A. Klipov, shows Ruslan just before he enters the palace to rescue his beloved. At the bottom of the painting, Chernomor sits on his throne holding court while his slaves tend to his long flowing white beard. In the third panel, painted by V. Brovkin, we see the lovers fleeing from the castle after Ruslan has vanquished the sorcerer with the aid of the sword given to him by the Giant Head. The same techniques and materials were used to paint this majestic work as were used by the Icon painters of the past.

Triptych. 93" x 53"

Inquiries should be addressed to: Siamese Imports Co., Inc., 450 West John St., Hicksville, NY 11801.

Library of Congress No. 89-92285
ISBN No. 0-940202-10-7
Printed in United States of America

Introduction

Just five days before this introduction was written, several of my colleagues and I sat by the shores of the Teza River, which flows through the forest surrounding the village of Palekh. We were leaving for Moscow the next morning and having a last picnic with some of the Palekh and Kholui painters and their families. After eating the black bread, boiled potatoes and delicious huge pickled mushrooms which had been picked in the spring in this very forest, the artists and their families serenaded us with old Russian folk songs.

As their beautiful voices and harmonies filled the air, I realized, once more, that no one else in the world could have painted the little boxes that for the past twenty two years I had traveled so many thousands of miles to obtain. These artists are deeply rooted in the very soil of Russia and their art is a continuation of the techniques and disciplines which were practiced for many generations before them.

As Nicolai Golikov, son of one of the founders of the Palekh School of Painting, and a renowned artist in his own right, sang of the love of a country boy and girl and their trials and tribulations, flashes of vignettes from various lacquer boxes which had passed through my hands over the years came to my mind and I saw the two lovers as they would have lived and passed their time here, perhaps walking in a forest such as this and singing the same songs in the same way as they were being sung this lovely late summer afternoon.

The time of Peristroika and Glasnost in the Soviet Union today is a very difficult time for all. New ideas, new freedoms and hopes for a new and better way of life for the people are sweeping through the land. But these upheavals bring with them many new difficulties as well, which will have to be coped with before the longed-for changes are realized.

As far as the artists are concerned, it is my fervent hope that the near future will bring them a new structure which will enable them to have a more comfortable and independent way of life and the ability to determine their own artistic futures.

When the Museum of Man invited me to take part in the Festival of Soviet Arts in San Diego from October 21st to November 11th, 1989, I greeted the proposal with great enthusiasm. I have worked with the Director of the Museum Shop, Shirley Phillips, for many years. She is a dear friend and a valued partner in my efforts in connection with the introduction of this art form to the American public.

The articles which are in this exhibit were acquired over a period of more than twenty years and represent works painted from 1924 to the present. Many of the pieces were commissioned for the publication of both the first and second volumes of my books "Russian Lacquer, Legends and Fairy Tales." Others were ordered and painted for my firm and retained for the collection because they were of such high caliber that I knew that they would some day be needed for just such a Museum exhibit. Numerous other works of great beauty and artistic value are now in the possession of many collectors in the United States who, I know, have great joy and satisfaction from the fact that these treasures are in their home and part of their lives.

Some of the pieces included in this exhibit, such as the boxes shown on pg. 33 are commissioned originals. Limited editions of these boxes were subsequently produced for us.

My only regret is that, because of the limitation of space, the works of many other superb painters could not be included in this exhibit.

I would like to take this opportunity to thank Dr. Douglas Sharon, the Director of the Museum of Man, for his sponsorship of the premiere showing of this collection. Deep appreciation also to Jane Smethurst, Joanne Heaney, Jeri Corbin, Donna Kindig and Linda Fisk for their enthusiastic and professional help in mounting this exhibit on such a high artistic level. From the first meeting we had, months ago, I felt that the collection would be in loving hands.

And now it remains only to welcome you, the viewer, into the land of fantasy—the land of the Masters of Russian Lacquer Miniature Painting.

Lucy Maxym
September, 1989

3

2. LUKOMORYA V. KOROVKIN 1988 PALEKH

Pushkin sits under a gnarled old tree. A magic cat, tied to the tree with a long golden chain, sits nearby and listens while the legends are unfolded. Surrounding the great story teller are elements from his wonderful epics. A Russalka reclines in the branches of the tree. Ruslan battles Chernomor while Ludmilla awaits her rescue in the palace. Firebirds roost in the branches. Baba Yaga rides in her mortar and pestle, home to her wooden hut which stands on chicken legs. Thirty three knights rise up out of the sea to guard Prince Gvidon's Magic City Prince Elisey asks the Sun to tell him where his beloved Princess can be found, while Koschei counts his golden treasures. One can also see the Enchanted Frog Princess, as well as the Magic Fish. In vignettes within the borders that encompass all sides are further symbols of the heroes and heroines of Pushkin's monumental tales.

Box. 10½'' x 8½'' x 3''

3. THE SEVEN SEMEONS   V. SMIRNOV   1985   PALEKH

*The nine panels on this chest contain incredibly detailed scenes from the story.
Numerous people, ships, castles, churches and animals inhabit this little masterpiece,
each with a role to play in the typically Russian tale.*

Persian chest, on legs. 3¾'' x 2¾'' x 3½''

4. THE SEVEN SEMEONS   V. SMIRNOV   1983   PALEKH

*This consumate miniaturist creates a magical composition in which the
entire story is told in a delightful and humorous way.*

Flat coffer with curved sides, on legs. 6½'' x 4½'' x 1½''

The untimely passing of Vladimir Smirnov in 1988 is mourned by all who loved and admired the man
and his art. He was certainly one of the greatest painters that Palekh has produced.

6

6. THE HUMPBACKED PONY   N. ZIMIN   1987   PALEKH

In olden days, salt was a precious commodity, often more precious than silver or gold. Salt cellars, in the form of a throne, were made of wood and other materials. Sometimes they were made of silver or gold, decorated with enamel and studded with precious stones. This salt cellar is such a precious article, lavishly decorated with many scenes from a much-loved fairy tale. The back contains a magnificent example of the technique of the Palekh border used at its most fanciful, with exotic birds incorporated into the gold, silver, red and blue composition.

Salt cellar in form of throne. 5" x 5" x 3½" x 8"

← 5. TRIUMPH OF LIGHT   A. KOCHUPALOV   1983   PALEKH

Excepts from the painter's thoughts about this composition: "The painter's philosophical and creative conception of this work is founded on the eternal battle between Light and Dark, Day and Night, Good and Evil and the birth of Truth.

All these elements are interpreted in an allegoric manner. The very concept of this painting is unique within the stylistic confines of Palekh Art. Night, with its' single candle, personifies the presence of dark forces and carries within itself the image of human tragedy — the fight between Life and Death.

As a contrast to the Warriors of the Night — the forces which try to prevent Night from disappearing forever — the heralds of Morning proclaim a new Day, gloriously rising over the entire agitated world. The new Day celebrates its victory and one can hear the music of Light, Life and Virtue.

But Night withdraws unconquered, unconquerable as Death itself. It will return again and again, and the battle between Light and Dark, Virtue and Evil, Truth and Dishonesty, Life and Death — it all starts again and continues eternally."

Mr. Kochupalov's work is greatly influenced by music. He states that he was under the spell of the Rachmaninoff Third Symphony at the time he painted this work.

Painting. 21½" x 15¾"

7. RUSLAN AND LUDMILLA V. FEDOTOV 1980 PALEKH

The top of the box depicts Ruslan and Ludmilla's Wedding Feast. The four sides recreate scenes between Ruslan and Chernomor, Ruslan and the Magic Head, the Battle of the Suitors and Ludmilla's rescue from the sorcerer's palace.

Box. 2½'' x 2½'' x 2''

8. RUSLAN AT CHERNOMOR'S CASTLE V. ZOLOTAREY 1979 PALEKH

After all his adventures, Ruslan finally arrives at the sorcerer's castle to rescue Ludmilla.

Box. 3½'' x 1¼'' x ½''

9. SCENES FROM RUSLAN AND LUDMILLA V. FEDOTOV 1975 PALEKH

The composition encompasses many scenes from the remarkable Pushkin epic: Chernomor, The Magic Head, Ludmilla, captive in the sorcerer's sumptuous palace, Ruslan riding to Ludmilla's rescue and the final celebration of Ruslan and Ludmilla's wedding feast.

Box. 10½'' x 8'' x 1¾''

10. THE PRINCESS AND THE SEVEN BOGATYRS   V. BARYNIN   1982   PALEKH

The Princess bids farewell to her protectors, the Seven Bogatyrs. Vignettes on the sides and top of the painting show her being taken into the forest, Prince Elisey searching for her and her rescue by her beloved.

Box. 7" x 5" x 1½"

11.   FIREBIRD   V. BROVKIN   1979   PALEKH

All the characters from this favorite story appear: Ivan and the Firebird, the Fair Elena, and the mysterious grey wolf. Superb flowering scrolls and borders further enhance the painting.

Box. 8" x 5" x 1½"

9

12. THE RAVEN   A. POCHANIN   1978   PALEKH

An old couple have three beautiful daughters. The eldest marries the Sun, the middle daughter marries the Moon, while the loveliest of them all — the youngest daughter — marries a handsome Raven. Swirling stars and constellations surround the Palace of the Sun and the Palace of the Moon. This painting was commissioned for the cover of the book "Russian Lacquer, Legends and Fairy Tales" Vol. I.

Painting. 15¾" x 8½"

13. SADKO   B. BARANOV   1977   PALEKH

Sadko finds himself in Neptune's Kingdom at the bottom of the sea. The sides of this lovely box are decorated with fanciful fish, seascapes and ships.

Box. 5'' x 5'' x 1½''

14. WEDDING FEAST   M. SHEMAROVA   1958   PALEKH

A beautifully executed composition. The Tsar sits on an intricately decorated throne, presiding over a grand wedding feast. Everyone gazes at the lovely bride who has just arrived. Food and drink abound. Musicians and jesters provide entertainment for the Tsar's guests.

Box. 10½'' x 8'' x 2½''

12

15. THE SEVEN SEMEONS O. MAKAROVA 1985 PALEKH

The seven brothers tell the Tsar of their adventures. There is an extremely delicate and intricate border enhancing the sides of this box.

Box. 8½'' x 6½'' x 1¾''

**16. THE PRINCESS AND THE SEVEN BOGATYRS
A. KUHARKIN   1985   PALEKH**

Scenes from the story are painted on top and in vignettes on the sides, surrounded with flowering borders.

Rounded oval box. 5¾'' x 2¼'' x 1½''

17. RUSALKA Z. VIUGINA 1975 PALEKH

A lyrical painting, utilizing blues and greens. It shows Rusalka rising up from the depths of the lake at the bidding of her lover, the Prince.

Box. 5¾'' dia. x 1¼''

18. VASILISA THE BEAUTIFUL   F. KRITOV   1980   PALEKH

Vasilisa stands before Baba Yaga's wooden hut, while the Knights of the Sun and the Night ride behind her. Exotic firebirds roost in the trees.

Box. 5" x 4" x 1"

19. THE ENCHANTED FROG PRINCESS   BURTSEVA   1979   PALEKH

On the cover we see the Frog Princess arriving at the Tsar's Feast. The rest of the story unfolds around the entire box.

Box. 3½" dia. x 1¾"

**20. THE ENCHANTED FROG PRINCESS
E. BOLSHAKOVA   1984   PALEKH**

Vasilisa makes swans appear at the Tsar's Feast, while her brothers and sisters-in-law watch in envy. The four sides of this box are highly ornamented.

Box. 2½" x 1" x 1¼"

21.   THE ENCHANTED FROG PRINCESS   A. KRAIKIN   1980   PALEKH

Vasilisa waves her hand and swans appear.

Box. 6½" x 2½" x 1¼"

14

22. BORIS GUDUNOV   A. ARAPOV   1985   PALEKH

This magnificent work traces the life of Boris from the time he presents himself to his people, who entreat him to become their Tsar. One side shows the old monk Pimenn inscribing the terrible events of the times in his Chronicles. The front panel teems with miserable people begging the Tsar for relief from their hunger and suffering. The back panel shows the Tsar comforting his wife and the young Tsarevich while his boyars watch with horror, realizing that madness has finally overcome their ruler. A powerful work.

Large treasure chest, on legs. 8" x 5¾" x 5¼

23. EUGENE ONEGIN   N. MICHAELOVA   1985   PALEKH

The entire story, written by Pushkin, upon which the opera of the same name is based, unfolds on the surfaces of this treasure chest. The interior scenes, as well as the architectural details are especially beautifully done.

Large treasure chest, on legs. 8" x 5¾" x 5¼"

24. CHURILLO PLENKOV   V. ABRAMOV   1979   PALEKH

"One day on the river called Saroga, strange people appeared. They broke our fishing boats. What to call them no one knows. Churillo, son of Plenkov, gathered his people to defend his land from these invaders": So reads the calligraphy on the cover of this box.

Box. 9¼" x 6½" x 1¾"

25. TROYKA   R. SMIRNOVA   1978   PALEKH

A man and his love sit in the sleigh, snugly swathed in furs, as the Troyka races through the swirling snow.

Painting. 13½" x 10¼"

16

26. THREE MAIDENS   V. BAKALOV   1979   PALEKH

*Tsar Saltan chooses for his Tsaritsa the Maiden who has
promised to love him and bear him a beautiful son.*

Plate. 10¼" dia.

**27. TSAR SALTAN   T. ANDRIYASHIKINA
1979   PALEKH**

*All elements of the story appear: The Magic Squirrel,
the Thirty-three Knights, the Swan changing into a
Princess, and finally, the happy reunion of Tsar Saltan
and his family.*

Box, with curved sides. 2" x 2" x 2"

28. TSAR SALTAN   O. AN   1975   PALEKH

*Tsar Saltan arrives at the Magic Island and is met by Prince Gvidon, his Swan Princess bride and Tsar Saltan's
long lost wife. The populace looks on as Chernomor leads his thirty three knights out of the sea. Beautifully
executed floral borders further enhance this work.*

Box. 9½" x 6¾" x 2¼"

Ludmilla, free to roam at will in the Sorcerer's garden, walks among majestic trees and blossoming shrubs. Peacocks and gentle deer walk beside her.

Plate. 8'' dia.

30. SCARLET FLOWER   Y. SHANITSIN   1984   PALEKH

Although this story is called ''Scarlet Flower'' in Russia, it is the same, in many respects, to the one which we know as ''Beauty and the Beast.'' Variations of this tale appear in the fairy tale lore of many countries.

Small treasure chest, green, on legs. 2½'' x 2'' x 2''

31. SILVER HOOF   V. KURBATOV   1984   PALEKH

When Silver Hoof leaps up on the roof and starts to tap his hoof — jewels come tumbling down for the grandfather and little Daria to gather.

Box. 4¾'' x 4¾'' x 1½''

32. DANCE OF THE GALAXIES   N. LOPATIN   1969   PALEKH

*Heavenly Horsemen gallop amidst a riot of stars and constellations which seem
to explode in all directions, running over from the top on to the sides of this
exciting work.*

Box. 7½'' x 3'' x 1½''

33. TSAR SALTAN   B. ERMOLAYEV   1975   PALEKH

*Thirty three knights rise up out of the sea, marching behind their leader,
Chernomor. They guard the city by night and go back to the sea by day.
The Magic City appears in the background.*

Box. 8'' x 5'' x 1¾''

34. TSAR SALTAN   V. FEDOTOV   1980   PALEKH

*Tsar Saltan dominates the composition. He is surrounded by vignettes showing scenes from
this powerful tale by Alexander Pushkin.*

Box. 10½'' x 8½'' x 1¾''

35. ILYA MUROMETZ   N. LOPATIN   1983   PALEKH

Ilya, the greatest of the Three Bogatyrs, vanquishes his nemesis, Solovey Razboynik. Alyosha Popovich and Dobrinya Nikitich ride to his aid.

Painting. 15½" x 8¾"

Палех 1983 г. Н.Лопатин

36. VASILISA THE BEAUTIFUL   A. Kuznetsov   1979   PALEKH

Vasilisa holds her little doll close for comfort as she stumbles on the tree roots and stumps in the dark forest. Baba Yaga's wooden hut, on chicken legs, stands nearby. The forest abounds with fantastic trees and foliage, vines twine on trees like snakes. The Horseman of the Day rides high in the sky, foretelling the break of dawn.

Painting. 12" x 7½"

37. BATTLE   I. GOLIKOV   1924   PALEKH

A fierce battle between the Mongol invaders and the defenders of Rus. Churches are shown in flames in background. This case was painted by one of the founders of the Palekh School of Miniature Painting.

Cigarette case. 5" x 3¼" x ¾"

38. BLACKSMITHS   N. GOLIKOV   1973   PALEKH

The middle panel of this box depicts blacksmiths hard at work. The sides show life in the village — a girl working a primitive tractor, boys on horseback in the forest with their bows and arrows. The beauty of the foliage and the exquisite stylized floral borders contrast with the obviously hard lot of the workers. This box was painted by the son of the founder of Palekh.

Box. 9¼" x 6¾" x 2¼"

39. WARRIOR — DEATH TO THE INVADERS
Y. GOLIKOV   1988   PALEKH

A mighty Bogatyr slays the Mongol invader. We see the grim subject mitigated by the idyllic sight of the golden sun rising over a wooden church and lighting up the golden crucifixes on the onion domes. Exquisite golden borders enhance the tops and sides of the box, which was painted by the grandson of Ivan Golikov.

Box. 8½" x 6" x 1¾"

40. SCARLET FLOWER S. ADEYANOV 1982 PALEKH

The top and all four sides depict scenes from the story. If one looks closely, one can see the Beast watching Beauty in his garden where the perfect scarlet flower grows.

Small treasure chest, red, on legs. 2½" x 2" x 2"

42. STEPAN RAZIN N. DENISOV 1984 KHOLUI

Stepan Razin spends months on a deserted island with his love, a beautiful Persian Princess, whom he will later cruelly fling to her death in the sea.

Cigarette case, red. 4¾" x 3¼" x 1¼"

**41. LUKOMORYA (PUSHKIN'S TALES)
     Y. VINOGRADOV 1985 PALEKH**

The Magic Cat sits in front of Pushkin, listening to him intently as he weaves his marvelous stories. Characters from these stories people all 9 panels of this gem of miniature art.

Persian chest, red, on legs. 4" x 3" x 3½"

43. THE SEVEN SEMEONS A. KURKIN 1985 PALEKH

The Seven Semeons sail away with the lovely princess while the Tsar and his retinue are left gazing after them on the shore.

Coffer, on legs, red, curved sides. 6½" x 4" x 1½"

44. THE SCARLET FLOWER   E. BOLSHAKOVA   1985

The Beast has been freed from the curse put on him by an enemy of his father and now he and the Maiden are shown together after their wedding. Her family strew flowers before them. The remainder of the box depicts various scenes from the story. This work is an outstanding example of the lyrical quality which this young woman brings to her art.

Large treasure chest, red, on legs. 8" x 5¾" x 5¼"

45. FIREBIRD   V. BUTORINA   1984

Ivan grasps a feather from the elusive Firebird. The garden around seems to explode in a riot of flowers.

Coffer, red, with curved sides, on legs. 6½" x 4" x 1½"

46. THE HUMPBACKED PONY   N. LOPATIN   1975   PALEKH
*The people watch in amazement as the Enchanted Pony and two magnificent steeds
fly through the air.*
Painting. 12" x 7½"

47. VASILISA   I. LIVANOVA   1985   PALEKH

Vasilisa leaves Baba Yaga's hut in the deep forest. Exquisitely detailed foliage covers all surfaces. The Horsemen of the Sun, the Moom, the Day and the Night are depicted on the four sides.

Rectangular chest, on legs. 2¾" x 2" x 2"

48. FIREBIRD   A. BAKALOV   1978   FALEKH

Prince Ivan watches as the Firebird soars into the Tsar's garden to eat the special apples growing there.

Box. 4" x 3" x 1¼"

49. VASILISA THE BEAUTIFUL
**   K. KUKULEYEVA   1985   PALEKH**

The top and 4 panels are painted with scenes from the story. The lower four panels are highly ornamented.

Persian chest, dark green. 3" x 2" x 3¼"

50. TEA PARTY   G. SHIRIAKOVA   1977   PALEKH

Four happy people sit around a samovar, drinking tea and eating pancakes. One of the girls gives a pancake to the cat to enjoy. We see the interior of a typical old Russian wooden house.

Box. 2¼" x 1¾" x 1"

51. GOING TO THE WELL   V. KARTASHOVA
**   1980   PALEKH**

Sunrise on a cold wintry day. The roofs of the wood huts of the village are covered with snow. A young girl trudges through ice covered streets to the communal well for water.

Box. 4" dia. x ¾"

52. THE SEVEN SEMEONS   B. VELICHKO   1987   PALEKH

*The seven brothers build a ship that is as beautiful as a palace and rides
the sea like a lively porpoise.*

Medium treasure chest, blue, on legs. 5" x 4" x 4"

53. TSAR SALTAN   O. GOLUBEV   1984   PALEKH

*Beautifully detailed paintings ending with the happy reunion of Prince Gvidon, his
Swan Princess Bride, Tsar Saltan and his long lost Queen at a grand feast in Gvidon's
palace within the Magic City.*

Medium treasure chest, red, on legs. 5" x 4" x 4"

54. TWELVE MONTHS   V. KONOVALOVA   1985   PALEKH

April hands a golden ring to the little girl, while all the other months look on. The border around the sides of the entire box is masterfully executed in gold and silver. There are baskets overflowing with snowdrops worked into this border.

Coffer, blue, with curved sides, button legs. 6½" x 4" x 1½"

55. TWELVE MONTHS   V. KURBATOV   1985   PALEKH

The little girl peeks from behind a tree, entranced at the sight of the twelve months of the year gathered in the glen before her. Snowdrops are incorporated into the border.

Box, blue, with curved sides. 5¾" x 2½" x 1¾"

56. TWELVE MONTHS   M. VESELOV   1984   KHOLUI

The Winter Months relinquish their rights to the Spring Months so that the maiden can gather snowdrops in January. All the months, animals and birds gather around the little girl as she fills her basket to overflowing. The border combines silver and gold.

Box, on legs. 6½" x 2½" x 1¼"

29

58. PUSHKIN AT MICHAELOVSKOYE   E. PECHKINA   1984   KHOLUI

Pushkin, now grown, once more sits with his old Nanny while she retells the legends and fairy tales she told him when he was a child. Her stories inspired him to write his masterpieces. If one looks closely at the roaring flames in the fireplace, one can see the forms of Ruslan and the Giant Head.

Box. 2½″ x 1¾″ x 1″

57. SIVKA BURKA   B. KHARCHEV   1983   KHOLUI

To the amazement of the Tsar and his people, Sivka Burka leaps so high that young Ivan is able to grasp the ring from the Tsarevna's hand.

Box, on legs. 6″ x 4″ x 1½″

59. THE SNOWMAIDEN   V. BLINOV   1971   KHOLUI

The Snowmaiden appears in front of the old couples' house and announces that she has come to be their longed for daughter. The girl of snow is dressed in a beautiful garment decorated with snowflakes and wears a crown of jewels on her lovely hair.

Box. 5¾″ x 5¾″ x 1½″

60. EMELYA AND THE MAGIC PIKE   L. ZVERKOVA   1985   PALEKH

Emelya catches a Magic Pike who promises him that his every wish will be granted if he throws him back into the water. The story is unfolded on all surfaces of the box.

Small treasure chest, blue. 3¾" x 2½" x 1½"

61. EMELYA AND THE MAGIC PIKE   V. BABKIN   1981   KHOLUI

The stove left the hut and arrived at the palace, with Emelya sitting on top, much to the surprise of the Tsar and his people and to the delight of the Princess, who watched from inside the palace. The ornamental border on this charming box is painted in gold and silver. The expressions on the faces of the characters show a master's hand at work.

Box. 11" x 8¼" x 1¼"

62. PUSHKIN IN THE FOREST   A. KOZLOVA   1986   FEDOSKINO

Pushkin, his walking stick and ever present sheets of paper at hand, interrupts his walk in a misty forest — perhaps to dream of yet another masterpiece.

Box. 6¾" x 1¾" x 4¼"

63. AFTER THE BATH   M. NOVIKOVA   1987   FEDOSKINO

A lovely girl bathes near the warm stove in her wooden home. An embroidered towel stretches out at her feet — her kitten waits contentedly. Another example of some artists' departure from the traditional Russian Lacquer subject matter.

Box. 6¾" x 1¾" x 1¼"

64. LANDSCAPE   Y. KARAPAEV   1984

The coming of spring brings the budding of the willows on the shores of a still frozen river.

Box, painted on mother of pearl. 3½" x 2¾" x 1½"

**65. LUBAVA   N. SOLONINFIN
1983   FEDOSKINO**

Faithful Lubava waits on the shore for Sadko's return. In the background are the magnificent churches of Novgorod.

Box, painted on mother of pearl. 2" x 3½" x 1"

**66. FEROPONTOV MONASTERY
S. KOZLOV   1984**

An outstanding architectural monoment from ancient times.

Box, painted on mother of pearl. 2½" x 3¼" x 1¾"

**67. NORTHERN SONG   Y. KARAPAEV
1972   FEDOSKINO**

In the golden northern light, the young people come out to sing and dance.

Box. 1½" x 1½" x ¾"

68. SCARLET FLOWER   N. ZOTOV   1963   FEDOSKINO

Painted over pure gold and silver leaf. As Beauty gazes at her lovely scarlet flower, picked from the Beast's enchanted garden, her two sisters revel in the silks and jewels brought back to them by their father.

Box, with legs. 4¾" x 4¾" x 3"

69. VOLNITSA   P. MITYASHIN   1984   KHOLUI

*Stepan Razin and his gang of brigands. This legend
of Razin, the first of the Don Cossacks, is retold
to this day. His life is the basis for popular songs
and literary works.*

Box. 4¼" x 3¾" x 1½"

70. STEPAN RAZIN   V. SEDOV   1983   KHOLUI
*The rogue, Stepan, organizes his gang of men for the raid in which he will capture
the Persian Princess.*

Box. 4¾" x 3½" x 1"

71. DANILO, MASTER CRAFTMAN   N. LAPSHIN   1984   KHOLUI

*After Danilo lives and works with the Mistress of Copper Mountain for many months in her malachite cavern, he can
finally carve the perfect stone flower. Now, when she has taught him all the secrets of precious stones, the Mistress,
realizing that she can never give him the human love which he needs, releases him and tells him to go back to his faithful
wife, Katya. The border on this box combines geometric and floral motifs, in gold, blue and red — symbolizing the
precious stones from the Mistress's kingdom.*

Box. 10" x 6¼" x 1½"

72. THE LIFE OF TSAR IVAN   KRILOV   1967   MSTERA

An incredibly detailed and technically magnificent work which chronicles the times of Ivan the Terrible. We see the architect of St. Basil's Cathedral, one of the wonders of the world to this day, begging for his life from the vengeful Tsar who, to make sure that the architect will never again build anything to rival this masterpiece, has him put to death. An entire army rides over the cobblestones of Moscow, one sees the inhuman acts which were perpetrated by the mad Tsar and the terror which the people felt in those days. All these emotions are interpreted through the technique of miniature painting by a consumate artist. One can look at this painting for hours, and through it be transported to the streets of Moscow and inside the rooms of the palace, as well as its dungeons, during the reign of Tsar Ivan.

Box. 9¾'' x 4½'' x 1½''

73. CHOOSING A BRIDE   V. KORSAKOV
1964   MSTERA

On the Tsar's orders, his three sons shoot an arrow into the air. Wherever the arrow lands is where each will find his wife. The arrow of the youngest son falls near a tiny frog!

Box. 2¾'' x 1¾'' x ½''

74. THE STONE FLOWER   A. BABURIN   1978   KHOLUI

The Mistress of Copper Mountain reveals the perfect stone flower to Danilo.
Box. 10'' x 6'' x 1½''

75. THE BATTLE OF 1223 AT THE KALKA RIVER   L. FOMICHEV   1965   MSTERA

Seemingly thousands of warriors are battling at the river's edge. One cannot get the sense of whether Rus or the Mongols are triumphing — only that it is a fierce and tragic scene. Reinforcements race up the river to join in the fray. Bows, arrows and spears fill the air, many finding their mark in human flesh.

Box. 9½'' x 7½'' x 1½''

76. THE HUMPBACKED PONY   L. FOMICHEV   1970   MSTERA

"Beyond the mountains, beyond the forests . . ." So starts the tale written in minute letters as a border around the entire top of this charming work.

Box. 12½'' x 7'' x 1½''

77. RUSLAN AND LUDMILLA   V. TIKHOMIROV   1980   MSTERA

A splendid work. Pushkin's epic story unfolds on top, front and sides of this superb cabinet. It contains two doors and three small drawers. In addition to the beautiful paintings, exquisite ornamentation adorns all surfaces.

Cabinet, on legs. 19" x 17" x 8"

78. RUSLAN AND LUDMILLA   V. TIKHOMIROV   1979   MSTERA

The top of the box depicts Ruslan's meeting with Finn. Vignettes amid the richly decorated backgrounds show Ruslan at various stages of the story, from his encounter with the Magic Head, to his battles with Chernomor and Ratmir and his rescue of Ludmilla.

Small Chest. 3" x 2½" x 2"

79. THE BUILDERS   V. MOSHKOVITCH   1978   MSTERA

On the cover, architects present models of a church which they wish to build for the Tsar. The process of building the wooden church, from the cutting of the logs on, is depicted around all sides.

Rectangular Chest, on Legs. 5" x 2¾" x 2¼"

80. THE FLYING SHIP   A. ZHEMANOV   1984   MSTERA

The Flying Ship soars off into the sky, to the amazement of the Tsar and his Tsaritsa.

Box. 4" x 3" x 1½"

81. FENIST THE FALCON   V. MOSHKOVITCH   1984   MSTERA

The Falcon flies out of the window before the maiden's father and sisters enter her room.

Box. 3¾" x 3¾" x 1½"

82. FORTUNE TELLING   V. MOSHKOVITCH
1984   MSTERA

Young girls tell their fortunes by floating wreaths of flowers on the river. Their sweethearts peek out from behind the trees.

Oval Box. 3½" x 2" x 1¼"

83. THE LEGEND OF PRINCE IGOR   E. SIVYAKOV   1987   PALEKH

Several surfaces are covered with graphic battle scenes. One panel depicts Igor's faithful wife, Yaroslavna, praying to the sun for her husband's safe return. The technically complicated borders combine pure gold with color. Entwined in the border on the top of the box are animals and battle scenes.

Large treasure chest, on legs. 8¾" x 6½" x 7¼"

39

84. THE PRINCESS AND THE SEVEN BOGATYRS   P. KOCHETOV   1987   PALEKH

On the top of the box, the Princess is shown greeting the Bogatyrs at the entrance to their house in the forest. On the left we see her stepmother gazing into her mirror to make sure she is the "fairest woman in the land." Encircling the entire box is the story from the time the Princess is taken into the forest until her rescue by Prince Elisey.

Box, 6'' dia. x 4¼''

85. SADKO V. VLESKO 1987 PALEKH

*An extraordinarily detailed work. In one scene, Sadko addresses the noblemen of Novgorod. In another, Sadko finds himself
on the ocean floor, in Neptune's kingdom, where he meets and falls in love with the Princess Volkhova.*

Large treasure chest, on legs. 8" x 5¾" x 5½"

86. OLD PALEKH, EGG ON STAND   E. SHANITSINA   1986   PALEKH

Encircling the egg are scenes from the Palekh of old, The famous Cathedral dominates the top of the composition, one farmer sows while another plows. A group of the famed wood carvers work on a new wooden house in the same way as had been done for centuries before. A young man meets his sweetheart at the village well. The stand for the egg is richly and completely ornamented in gold. One of three eggs commissioned in 1986.

Egg. 3½" Tall — Stand: 4½" Dia.

87. BATTLE   A. ARAPOV   1988   PALEKH

Ancient history and battles are favorite subjects for Palekh and Mstera painters. In this magnificent composition, the Bogatyrs, defenders of ancient Rus, fend off the Mongol invaders. The fierceness of the battle is once more mitigated by the beauty of the golden scroll work into which birds and animals are entwined.

Box. 10¾" x 4" x 3¾"

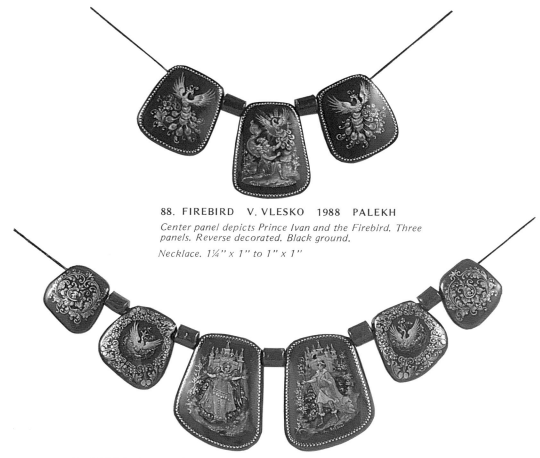

88. FIREBIRD   V. VLESKO   1988   PALEKH

Center panel depicts Prince Ivan and the Firebird. Three panels. Reverse decorated. Black ground.

Necklace. 1¼" x 1" to 1" x 1"

89. TSAR SALTAN   V. VLESKO   1989   PALEKH

On the two center panels, Prince Gvidon and his Swan Princess stand before the Magic City. The panels decrease in size. Reverse of each panel decorated with intricate floral scroll work. Cinnabar ground.

Necklace. 1½" x 1" to ¾" x ½"

90. TROYKA   R. BELOUSOV 1983   PALEKH

Pendant, framed in 14K gold.

1¾" dia.

91. FIREBIRD   A. NICOLAEV 1988   PALEKH

Pendant, framed in 24K gold over sterling, with genuine sapphire and five rose diamonds.

1¾" dia.

92. KONOK-GARBUNOK   V. YUSKOV 1988   PALEKH

Pendant, framed in 24K gold over sterling, with garnet.

1¾" dia.

93. TROYKA   T. ANDRIYASHKINA   PALEKH

The ubiquitous Palekh troyka.

Box. 3½" x 1¼" x 1¼"

94. SNOWMAIDEN   G. KUZMENKO   ca. 1980   PALEKH

We follow the Snowmaiden from the time she leaves Fairy Spring and Father Frost to join the human world, until she melts in the sun.

Box. 1½" dia. x 1¾"

95. THE VIRGIN OF VLADIMIR   NOT SIGNED
1975

*This lovely box is unsigned since it was painted during
a time in the Soviet Union when religious painting was
frowned upon. It is painted in the same manner as were
the old Icons, by an artist quite familiar with and
versed in the art of iconography.*

Box. 10" x 7½" x 1½"

96. THE VIRGIN OF VLADIMIR
PAINTER UNKNOWN

*Goldplated risa over completely painted Icon,
wIth intricate enameled crown. Late 18th —
early 19th century.*

Icon. 46" x 36"

44

97. MISTRESS OF COPPER MOUNTAIN   1989   PALEKH

The plaque which adorns the top of this jewelry box of speciman malachite was painted by E. Zhiriakova. We see the Mistress of Copper Mountain and Danilo sitting in the Malachite Cave. Serpents, lizards and snakes — denizens of the cavern—surround the Malachite Lady and seem to be listening intently as she explains the secrets of precious stones to the young lad.

Jewelry box, lined with brocade, on goldplated silver legs. 8¾" x 6" x 4"

Lucy Maxym has been largely responsible for the introduction of Russian Lacquer Miniature Painting to the United States and the rest of the world and for its development over the past two decades into an important twentieth century art form.

She has written two books on "Russian Lacquer Legends and Fairy Tales" and has edited and published "The History and Art of the Russian Icon from the X to the XX Centuries."

98. IVAN AND MARIA—LOVERS   L. FOMICHEV   1961   MSTERA

A pastoral scene. A boy and girl meet on a spring day. Maria has flowers entwined in her hair. Her mother and aunt watch in the background.

Box. 5½" x 3¾" x 1½"

99. LANDSCAPE   A. KOZLOVA   1983   FEDOSKINO

A serene Russian landscape, in early spring, when the ice on the river is beginning to break up.

Box, painted on mother of pearl. 2¾" dia.

100. OLD TOWN   N. SOLONINKIN   1984   FEDOSKINO

A complex of ancient churches and monasteries on the shores of a river.

Box painted on mother of pearl. 2½" x 3" x 1½"

101. ST. BASIL'S CATHEDRAL   V. SVYATCHINKOV   1987   FEDOSKINO

The use of mother of pearl brings new beauty to this interpretation of the ever fascinating domes and spires of one of the wonders of the world.

Painted on mother of pearl. 10" x 7¼" x 3"

102. KIRILOV MONASTERY   S. KOZLOV   1984   FEDOSKINO

Rocks of pure gold line the path to the Monastery.

Box. 7" x 7" x 2"

103. THREE MAIDENS   1972   FEDOSKINO

Three young girls spin and gossip. This composition has been widely reproduced over the years.

Box. 4" x 3½" x 1"

104. PRINCE IGOR   SKRIPUNOV   1980   FEDOSKINO

Yaroslavna and her attendants pray for the safe return of Prince Igor.

Box. 6¼" x 4¼" x 1¾"

105. THE TSAR MAID   A. KUZNETSOV   1973   FEDOSKINO

Ivan presents the Tsar Maid to the Tsar and the Court.

Large treasure chest, with rounded sides, on legs. 10¼" x 7½" x 3½"

106. KREMLIN   P. PUCHKOV   1974   FEDOSKINO

The painter shows the churches and buildings in the Kremlin on the surfaces of this tiny box.

Box 1½" x 1½" x ¾"

107. KONOK GARBUNOK   A. KUZNETSOV   FEDOSKINO

The horses' manes and the Tsar's garments take on an entirely new dimension when painted on mother of pearl.

Box. 3½" x 2½" x 1"

108. MASLENITSA   S. DMITREEV   1987   KHOLUI

People — young and old — gather around for a gay winter holiday. They build a snowman with a carrot for a nose and wear outlandish masks. The entire box is painted with scenes of merry making, courting, gathering around a Samovar and eating pancakes with tea — a traditional part of this holiday. The borders incorporate blue snowflakes within the golden ornamentation.

Small chest, with legs. 2¼" x 2" 1¼"

109. FAREWELL TO DOBRINYA   1984   KHOLUI

His Lady bids farewell to Dobrinya, the mighty Bogatyr, as he leaves to do battle with the Dragon, symbol of the Invaders of Russ.

Box. 2¾" x 2¼" x 1¼"

110. OLEG THE WISE   STEPANOV   1972   KHOLUI

Oleg stands before the skull of his beloved horse. The legend has it that a soothsayer's prophecy that the horse will cause his death is fulfilled when a snake slithers out of the skull and kills Oleg.

Box. 19" x 6" x 1½"

111. SNOWBELLS   V. STARKOVA   1961   MSTERA

A young girl brings food to her love, who has been waiting for her under an apple tree.

Chest. 2¾" x 2¾" x 2½"

112. MOROZKO AND FATHER FROST   A. SHADRIN   1961   MSTERA

Father Frost comforts Morozko, who has been left to die in the depths of the forest. Whimsical birds and other creatures look on.

Box. 4¼" x 3" x 1¼"

113. LOVERS MEETING   V. GLOTOV   1961   MSTERA

Lovely lyrical painting which is typical of the painting by Mstera Masters.

Box. 4¼" x 4¼" x 2"

114. SIVKA BURKA   T. STRUNINA   1984   MSTERA

The magic steed appears from nowhere and leaps up to the top of the tower where the Princess waits.

Box. 7" x 5¾" x 1½"

115. PRINCE IGOR   L. FOMICHEV   1965   MSTERA

Prince Igor is shown in the camp of Khan Kontchak. Although he is given every comfort and girls are sent to dance for him, he dreams only of escape and return to his faithful Yaroslavna.

Box. 5¼" x 3¾" x 1½"

116. TROYKA   V. MOSHKOVITCH   1982   MSTERA

On the top is a troyka, with three prancing horses. Encircling the entire box is a wintry landscape through which the horses must travel.

Cylinder box. 2¾" dia. x 3"

117. SCARLET FLOWER   A. KUHARKIN   1984   PALEKH

Beauty strolls in the glade of the Beast's magnificent gardens, surrounded by flowers and the songs of birds. The sides of this little box are intricately bordered in gold, carrying out the floral motif of the gardens.

Small chest, blue, on legs. 2½" x 1¾" x 1¾"

118. SUMMER   A. KOCHUPALOV   1987   PALEKH

Gently scalloped top and curved sides. One can almost feel the languid heat of summer. A shepherd sleeps under a tree, women are picking mushrooms in the nearby forest, others rest by the water. An example of the lyrical side of this artist's work, reflecting his love of the Russian countryside.

Chest, on legs. 5" x 4" x 3½"

119. THE FISHERMAN AND THE MAGIC GOLD FISH   L. DUKHANINA   1986   PALEKH

The old woman, now wealthy beyond all possible dreams, orders her old husband to be banished from her presence. From their original poverty, to riches, and then back to poverty again — all because of the limitless greed of the old woman.

Plate. 9½" dia.

120. MISTRESS OF COPPER MOUNTAIN   N. FEDOTOVA   1977   PALEKH

The lovely Rusalka, green as the ocean in which she lives, rises above the water to be with her love.

Box. 2½" dia. x ¾"

121. TROYKA   F. KRITOV   1978   PALEKH

Pendant, framed in 14K gold.

Rectangular. 2" x 1¼"

122. LUDMILLA AND CHERNOMOR   A. KOVALEV   1989   PALEKH

Flexible wood bracelet. Black ground.

2¾" dia. x ¾"

123. STEPAN RAZIN   A. ARAPOV   1982   PALEKH

The sea broils, reflecting the cruelty of the scene as Stepan Razin flings his love, the beautiful Persian Princess, into the sea to satisfy the demands of his gang of brigands.

Box. 5" x 4" x 1"

124. THE PRIEST AND HIS SERVANT BALDA   V. LEBEDEV   1988   PALEKH

Pushkin sits under a tree, quill in hand and paper by his side, as his story unfolds before him and all around the sides of this box.

Box. 8¼" x 5¾" x 3"

(Continued)

125. TROYKA   NOT SIGNED   ca. 1900

An example of the work done by the Lukutin establishment at the end of the 19th century. The lacquer available to these artisans was such that the examples of their work which has survived are almost completely crazed on the surfaces. At this point, they resemble very old leather.

Chest. 5¼" x 3½" x 3"

126. ST. SERGIUS   NOT SIGNED   ca. 1965

The life of Sergius of Radonezh is depicted on top and sides. This box was probably painted in Mstera.

Chest. 2¼" x 2" x 2"

127. VZGRANIE   E. NEZHEGORODOVA   1988

An example of the new Iconography now being painted in the Soviet Union by independant artists.

Box. 6¾" x 4¼" x 2½"

128. ICON, THREE PRELATES: IONNE ZLATOUST, ST. GREGORY, ST. VASILY   PAINTER UNKNOWN

Late 18th to early 19th century. This icon is especially interesting since it shows the traditional ornamentation of the garments which one can see today in the Russian Lacquer boxes being painted in Palekh and Kholui.

Icon. 11¾" x 13¾"

129. ICON, VIRGIN OF KAZAN

Early 18th Century.
Icon. 10½" x 12¼"

130. ICON, VIRGIN OF KAZAN

18th Century.
Icon. 9½" x 11½"

Photography by Diversified Photo Services, Plainview, New York 11803
Design and Typography by Free-Time Graphics, Inc., Oakdale, New York 11769
Printing by Frank C. Toole & Sons, Inc., Farmingdale, New York 11735